in love with you...

Cover Design: TreManda Pewett
Editor: Sarah Plamondon

ISBN-13: 978-0-9974265-7-1

Jeanius Publishing LLC
430 Lee Blvd
Lehigh Acres, FL 33936

For more information, please visit:
Pierrealexjeanty.com

Every page is dedicated to you,
My beautiful wife,

"Inspired"

You, my love, the beholder of my heart,
are my greatest inspiration;
the reason I have become
this kind of man.

You are the reason I am living this life
that I could've never imagined.
Before you, I was a boy with a numb heart,
watching time pass as I searched for passion.

You came in and blew down
the walls around my heart,
showed me how to be vulnerable
even from the start.
Of our conversations,
I knew there was nothing missing.

I saw beauty I had never known
swimming in your eyes, and
that is when I knew that one day
I would make you my wife.

Here you are loving me,
being the type of woman who helps me discover
the better me.

"What You Mean to Me"

You mean the world to me.
Without you, my world was black & white.
It was colorless,
the epitome of plain.
The storms were never followed by rainbows,
the birds never chirped beautifully,
and the sunshine stayed away from me.
But with you, I've learned to see gray.
I've gained sight to see the beautiful things in this
world,
beautiful things in others,
even beautiful things in myself.
People say you don't need anyone in this life,
but those are words of people who never had a
lover like you,
speech of people who never saw a love like ours.
Baby, I need you in my world.
Baby, I can't be a king without my queen.

"Addicted to You"

Love visited me when our eyes first met,
but I didn't know it until our hearts kissed.
I found reasons to stay in your smile,
and reason to make being in love a habit
in your soul.
Baby, you are my favorite drug.

"Staring"

There are times I stare at you and wonder how
blessing and luck came together
and convinced this miracle to happen.
I stare intricately,
cherishing every breath of you,
appreciating your existence,
soaking in your beauty.
I replay our greatest days and think about the life I
had without you.
A nightmare it was, though I always dreamt of
being in love.
Life for me didn't exist without you.
I was just surviving.
You've given me every reason to live.

"Faithfully Yours"

Forever isn't just a word, but our destination.
I am here to behold you until death makes us its
patient.
Love, I just love loving you.
To be the lover of a woman like you
is more than a dream come true.
I have been a fool who lost a good woman before
a great woman like you, and I will never jeopardize
and give you reason to close the door
on what we have.
My eyes are set on you,
I do not have another better half.
There may be other women out there in the eyes
of others who can compare,
but to me, to do so is a foolish dare.
How beautifully designed you are to me is proof
that God created us in pairs.
There's no wandering of my eyes
or curiosity in my bones.
This love for you I am here to water, and make
sure it never gets old.
I am yours forever,
despite what season, no matter the weather.

"Elevated Me"

I am on cloud nine with you,
and this is long after infatuation.
This is way beyond our first wave of obsession.
You've built a stairway with your encouragements,
paved them with uplifting words,
while dusting me of doubt.
Failure is nothing but a fading echo
with you by my side.
You've seen versions of me that
I had to be convinced existed,
strength in me that I didn't know
was buried there.
I have become so much more with you.

"It Hurts"

It hurts knowing that you've been hurt,
mistreated, betrayed, misled, and even abused.
How could someone find it right to do you wrong?
How could someone mishandle a heart so
precious?
I watch tears of joy leak out of your eyes when you
talk about how good I am to you.
I've shed tears myself thinking about how bad they
were to you.
I know I cannot focus on the past, but it hurts
knowing that I couldn't protect you then.
I sometimes wish I could've been there sooner.
Maybe if I had, you wouldn't be this strong woman
and me, this loving man.
Either way, it breaks my heart to know that people
found ways to commit evil to an angel like you,
although you haven't always been a saint.
I promise to never be any of those people who
committed those sins against you.
I am here to help you put those memories in the
past.

I was once asked, "What's your type?"

My answer was, "My wife."

"Past tense"

Your past is just a blur to me.
I have asked about it only to know both
the most beautiful things that ever took place,
and the ugliest things you've had to live through.
I am here to love who you are now,
and who you will become.
Neither will I ever to judge what you are no longer.
It makes me smile to see you proudly say,
"I am not this girl anymore."
You boldly proclaim the woman you are becoming
and vow never turn back into that misguided girl
again.
I am proud of who you've become.
You have every reason to be as well.

"Always Beautiful"

You are always beautiful in my eyes.
When I said "I do,"
I knew your body would change,
I knew that I would meet things I'd dislike, and
I knew our kisses would not always
taste the same.
I knew arguments would find their way to our lips,
I knew there would be cold seasons,
and great reasons for us to fall would spring up.
I did not fall in love with your body only,
I did not fall in love with your good words only,
I did not fall in love with your loving ways only,
I fell in love with all of you.
Despite how ugly things may get,
you will always be beautiful to me.

"Forever Grateful"

There are times I don't thank you enough,
but baby, I'm forever grateful for you.
There are times you feel like you don't do enough,
but baby, you've done so much
for me and our little family.
There are times you feel you haven't accomplished
enough.
I understand.
I will be by your side for you to accomplish more,
but baby, being a wife, a mother, a God-fearing,
loving, hardworking woman is more than enough
accomplishment.
Things many can't juggle, you balance so well.

"I Love You"

I said *"I love you"* quite a few times before you,
yet
none of them carried as much meaning as every
single one I've said to you.
Even when it's out of routine, being playful, or to
end a misunderstanding,
every part of my heart gets involved when I say it
to you.
I have found myself loving you in circumstances I
couldn't drag myself to love other people through.
This love is real,
this love is true,
this love is felt.

"Bffs"

There's no better friend than you.
You've been the beholder of my greatest secrets
since we met.

There is nothing in my past, present or future that
you will never know,
even the parts of me that have never been shown
to the other people on this earth who know me
best.
We are one, so I cannot see myself pouring some
and leaving the rest.
No matter what I need to get off my chest,
your ears will always be the place for them to rest.

"Take It or Leave It."

They say you shouldn't share too much when you
first meet someone.
Their reasoning is that if the person knows the ugly
things about you, they may easily walk away…
the exact reason why we told each other our worst
within our first two conversations.
We both pulled every bone from the skeletons in
our closets and threw them out, saying, "Here is
my worst, you can accept it or leave."
Man, did we feel free,
carrying no pretense in our voices
or holding back too much on our tongues.
I loved how we built on raw honesty.
This is how we've been able to build such a strong
foundation.

"Proud"

I will never be good at showing you off.
I have grown to be very humble
and sometimes too nice,
but being yours is one of the things
I am the proudest of.
I find random reasons to mention your name in
conversations, and
I give you credit for things you have no idea
happened in my life.
There's a joy in me that erupts when you are by
my side.
Baby, you will never be merely jewelry on my arm.
You will always the heart of my soul.

"Did You Know?"

Did you know that my favorite thing about you is that innocent smile that shows up on your face when I tell you how much I am in love with you?

Did you know that the thought of being with someone else never found its address with me?

Did you know that my other favorite thing about you is when you talk about spending time with God and growing in your faith? What more can a man have than a woman who strives to be a powerhouse spiritually?

Did you know that I am still amazed at how you raised Eli on your own, being both mom and dad before you met me?

Did you know I annoy you sometimes to make you mad, because there's nothing cuter to me than to watch you try to stay mad at me when you can't?

Did you know that one of the hardest things for me to do now would be to name a few of my exes, as your existence is slowly wiping them all out of my memory?

Did you know that I look forward to being old with you, traveling the world, listening to soul music, and making jokes with you about things people don't think we should laugh about?

Your smile will always have its way

of lighting up my world.

Your existence will always captivate me.

You are such a unique phenomenon.

"Safety"

I have found loyalty like yours nowhere else.
With you,
my heart is the safest it has ever been and the
safest it will ever be.
I can't bring myself to picture you betraying me,
neither do I believe that you could.
Forgiveness is always at the edge of your tongue,
ready to dive into whatever troubles us and bury it
in the past.
I married you because I believed that only death
would have the power to make you walk away from
me.
I saw endurance in you,
I smelled perseverance on you,
And you have proven yourself since.
How much easier it is to love someone whom you
know has your heart's best interest.

"Goofballs"

As I was growing up,
I was the secure child who hated jokes,
hated being made fun of.
Here with you, your play is the funniest thing to
me.
How you talk about my height,
the way you memorize my hand gestures when I
am mad,
and the way you make jokes about my manners.
The clumsy things you do,
the pure randomness, and your corny ways will
never stop creating memories for us to talk about.
You are both my wife, and my silly girlfriend.
The laughs you pull out of me are my favorite.
I am grateful for the entertainment that comes with
doing life with you.

"Peculiar Woman"

You've allowed me to be the man of the house,
the leader of the family,
something that is uncommon and hated in this
day.
Countless times we've had conversations where
you told me how you had no trust in men before
you put your trust in God,
how you played them when they couldn't get
serious.
You found strength in being independent because
none of them were ever dependable.
But now that you've met a man who would lay his
life down for you.
With me you've let go of that life,
and joined one you've never known.
I will never abuse this position, baby, it is an honor
to lead you and to make sacrifices for us.

"Breathtaking"

You may never understand this,
but when I hear you talk about chasing sunsets
and the beauty in the sun rising,
I will never be too impressed,
because you are far more beautiful to me.
I can watch you day and night.

"Super Mom"

I thought you were a great mother when I met you.
I exchanged my thoughts for believing that you are
an amazing mother when I see him excelling.
I exchanged my thoughts once again for knowing
that you are a phenomenal mother when I saw you
carry life in you for 9 months to a scary,
yet beautiful ending.
You naturally pushed through unimaginable pain to
introduce our daughter to this world.
I held your hand and practiced the breathing,
pushed with you, but never could I carry such pain
with you.
The night our daughter was born, I realized how
much stronger a woman can be than a man in
many areas.
What a mighty woman you are.
My love, you are a warrior.

You will never get lost in my shadow.
You are more than the wife of an author,
you are a queen with her own pen.

"Hear You Out"

I don't always hear you,
but I am always listening.
I may not always be open to hearing you out,
but listening to you is never a closed door.
Sometimes I am not focused,
but I consciously catch words.
Sometimes I don't pick up every sentence,
but I do my best to pick up the overall message
and give you a response.
I may laugh when you say, "One last thing," as
you continue to tell me stories when it's past my
bed time,
but I will always make an attempt to take in
everything you have to share with me.

"Apple of My Eyes"

It will always be easy for people to lose focus on what matters when they don't often take a hard look at what they have.

I know what I have, and I want to have it forever. Your smile, your dedication, the way you care for me, the way you love, our special moments, all are things I am not willing to jeopardize for excitement and attention from somewhere else.

You will never find me trying to find another woman. **For the rest of my life, I want to keep finding a new woman in you.**

"Protecting Us"

As of now, I've become a bully to temptation.
Every time I see it,
I ball up my fist and go after it.
I am not trying to be its friend.
In an over sexualized generation,
it has done nothing good for love stories.
It won't grab ours, and I won't be another man
who fails because he claims he is imperfect.
I will beat temptation to death before it comes to
take the life of our relationship.

"Uncommon Numbers"

They think all men fall into temptation. This is why they are quick to say, "*Wait till you are together for years before you say you will never get tired of her,*" clueless to the fact that I am falling more and more in love with you as more years are added on.

These are the same type of people who whispered, *"You're moving too fast,"* when I proposed to you 4 months after meeting you.

The same type of people who thought you were foolish to relocate far away with your son, to be with a man you'd known for 8 months.

The same people who told me it was silly to let you sleep alone in a place I'd provided for, with the mindset that I could only move in and be with you starting the night we were married.

The same people who thought I was crazy for marrying you 11 months after meeting you.

It's uncommon to them. Our story is uncommon, but that's what makes it so beautiful. We kept doing it the way they aren't used to.

"You Go Girl"

Baby, you're a champion.
You've lost many times,
but have seen plenty of "wins."
You've fallen so many times, but now you've
grown "wings."
You are powerful, my love.
When you wonder about your life, I want you to
know that you've been placed on this earth by the
Lord above.
In you, there's so much purpose,
your heart of gold that could never be purchased.
Don't you ever,
for a second,
think that you are worthless.
The chosen can never be.

"Healing"

To know what you've endured, but now see how
you are freely loving, is beautiful.
It's proof that healing is a medicine that is worth
chasing after your whole life.
Many have been hurt and became that hurt, but
you, you gained the courage to crawl your way out
of that mountain of pain.
You handed your hand to God and asked Him to
help you out.
You fought hard against the pain trying to keep
itself glued to you.
You broke free, baby.
There may be residue, but you broke free, baby.
Please, be proud of that.

"Moments"

The moments we laughed can never be compared
to the moments we cried.
The times we celebrated will always be far more
than the times we were conflicted.
There's more good in us being together, despite
the bad.
This,
this is love.
This is imperfect people perfectly loving one
another.
We have stored more smiles than we have created
frowns, and
we have held onto peace more than we've kept
our fists tightly holding onto selfishness.
This is love.
This is people in love fighting for love.

"Give You the World"

I have a habit of overworking.
As a man who grew up with nothing, when my
opportunity finally came, I couldn't help but take
advantage of every minute of it.
Now,
it is for you, it is for our kids, it is for our future.
My labor is pulling everything out of me that I can
give this world, to give you a world that will not rob
us of our sanity, our joy, and our peace.
I've heard many marriages fail because of
finances, and I know it won't happen to us, but I
never want lack to ever take anything away from
you and me.
You know my long hours are devoted, because I
am first passionate about what I do, but they are
devoted for you too.

"Seeing Love"

Let's be the example of love that our kids never
forget, even when they haven't had the best luck
in finding love.
Let's show them that heartbreaks aren't all that
exist in this world.
Let's be the hope they don't often see.
Let's be the family they aspire to have.
Let's be the best we can be,
not only for us, but for them.

"How To Keep a Man"

I did not have to see you naked
to fall for you.
I never had to make love to you
to be in love with you,
and now I am in love with you.
Nothing you take from me can take that away.

You deserve everything,

not because you ask for nothing, as they say,

but because you should have everything

good this life has to offer.

I will make sure of it.

"Daddy Duties"

There are many things I grew up without learning,
many things I should've been taught about being a
man that I was clueless to, until facial hair began
to sprout from my skin.
One of those things is being a father.
I've observed very few good fathers,
and known far too many children whose fathers
were only a man whom their mothers once knew.
Here I am, trying to become the very thing I've had
no training in,
yet here you are cheering me on,
encouraging me every step of the way,
giving me credit for every ounce of effort.
I thank you for thanking me for being the best
father that I know how to be.
You are making me a better father.

"Till Death"

And baby, I won't leave because you change.
That's what humans are supposed to do.
When it's for the better, I will grow with you,
and when it's for the worse, I will keep prayers on
my tongue and patience on my mind.
When I said, "*Till death do us part,*"
I was letting you know that I would do whatever it
takes to stay by your side.

"Freckle Face"

On some days,
your face is like the night sky with the brightest
stars glued to it,
and on other days,
beach sands with diamonds strategically placed.

"Communicate"

You un-purposely hurt me.
I shut down and let my sarcasm fight for me.
You get upset, all clueless.
We find ourselves on this couch again, resolving
this issue,
pouring our feelings out to find our wrong turns so
that we don't end up on this path again.
I know this is new to you, but this is new to me as
well.
I used to run away from my problems, but with
you, I don't want them to be unsolved.
I don't want them to give birth to bigger problems.
Let's never get away from handling our hard times
like adults.
Immaturity only causes more damage.

"Your Groupie"

I need you to keep on searching for your purpose,
keep on holding to your future goals.
I am pregnant with support,
and am more than willing to invest in your dreams.

"Conqueror"

Even when I die, I want what's left of me in your
memory to keep beating to death any insecurities
that may be left in you,
reminding you that you are beautiful as you are,
intelligent as you are,
powerful as you are,
chosen as you are.

If my heart had lips,

it would kiss you every minute.

If it had a voice,

it would over express how much you mean to

me.

Since it has neither,

it only beats for you.

"Misfit"

As normal goes out of style,
you refuse to follow the wave that views morality
as secondary to open mindedness.
Godly women like you are important seeds to this
earth.
I cannot wait to see the impact that branches out
of you.
I am dying to see the other fruits you will bear.

"Decisions"

I would rather work my butt off to give you the
world, for you to be home, being a mom, and
guiding our children.
But if that's not what you want for you,
then it's not what I want for you.
I want for you whatever you want for yourself.

"Habits"

I once thought my sarcasm to be one of my
greatest strengths.
With you, it is one of my greatest weaknesses. I
do not like how it makes you feel.
I had not always seen the side effects because it
was always second nature to me, but now I hate it.
I am working graveyard shifts to bury it.
I will crucify it for you.

"Watering My Roots"

Compliments from your lips used to be the hardest
things to receive.
They brought great discomfort to me, as
I've always been more familiar with negative
words.
They were my fuel for everything,
so many people who doubted me and said what I
was not, mocked me.
Now here you are, pointing out things about me
that I'd never seen as great, and you see them as
an accomplishment, as beautiful, worthy of
applause.
Now, I am embracing your words.
Now, I am beginning to believe you.
Now, I am gaining the strength to let those
compliments fly out of my own mouth as well.
Your patience is so appreciated, dear.

"Honored"

I'm glad I became the man whose eyes were made
to cherish everything that you are.

Even when my prose and poems aren't all
about you,
you are still my influence and my favorite of
them all.

It only took 3 days to write this. This is in between us moving to our new house, managing the business, taking the boys to practice & games, etc.
This is a small project to attach to our journey into a new home, and the beginning of new memories. This is also meant to be an appetizer to our readers before my next book.
If I took any longer to write this, my fingers would grow tired before my mind is emptied of the things I want to say about you. I would have a novel! But here I am, trying to make sure you don't see this, while I only scratch the surface about how much you mean to me.

Hope you love this baby,
I love you.

− Your husband.